Gone Forever!
Tyrannosaurus Rex

Rupert Matthews

Heinemann Library
Chicago, Illinois

HIGHLAND PARK PUBLIC LIBRARY

© 2003 Heinemann Library
a division of Reed Elsevier Inc.
Chicago, Illinois

Customer Service 888-454-2279
Visit our website at www.heinemannlibrary.com

All rights reserved. No part of this publication may be reproduced or transmitted in any form or by any means, electronic or mechanical, including photocopying, recording, taping, or any information storage and retrieval system, without permission in writing from the publisher.

07 06 05 04
10 9 8 7 6 5 4 3 2

Design by Ron Kamen and Paul Davies & Associates
Illustrations: by Maureen and Gordon Gray, James Field (SGA), and Darren Lingard
Originated by Anbassador Litho Ltd
Printed and bound in China by South China Printing Company

07 06 05 04
10 9 8 7 6 5 4 3 2

Library of Congress Cataloging-in-Publication Data
Matthews, Rupert.
  Tyrannosaurus rex / Rupert Matthews.
      p. cm. -- (Gone forever)
Includes index.
Summary: Describes the physical characteristics of Tyrannosaurus rex,
probably one of the very last dinosaurs on Earth, and discusses where it
lived.
  ISBN 1-40340-793-2 (HC), 1-4034-3421-2 (Pbk)
  1. Tyrannosaurus rex--Juvenile literature. [1. Tyrannosaurus rex. 2.
Dinosaurs.] I. Title. II. Gone forever (Heinemann Library)
  QE862..S3 M3326 2003
  567.912'9--dc21
                          2002004032

Acknowledgments
The author and publishers are grateful to the following for permission to reproduce copyright material:
pp. 4, 12, 22, 24 Francois Gohier/Ardea; p. 6 Geoscience Features Picture Library; pp. 8, 18, 20 Natural History Museum, London;
p. 10 Science Photo Library; p. 14 Corbis; p. 16 C. P. George/Visuals Unlimited; p. 26 Field Museum, Chicago.
Cover photo reproduced with permission of Corbis.

Special thanks to Dr Peter Mackovicky for his review of this book.

Every effort has been made to contact copyright holders of any material reproduced in this book. Any omissions will be rectified in subsequent printings if notice is given to the publishers.

Some words are shown in bold, **like this.** You can find out what they mean by looking in the glossary.

Contents

Gone Forever!

Sometimes, all the animals of one kind die. This means they become **extinct.** Scientists study extinct animals by digging for **fossils.** Fossils are found in rocks.

About 68 to 65 million years ago, animals were very different from those living today. Most of the animals that lived then have become extinct. One of these animals was a **dinosaur** called Tyrannosaurus rex.

Tyrannosaurus Rex's Home

Some scientists study rocks. They have studied rocks in which Tyrannosaurus rex **fossils** were found. They have used the rocks to find out about the area where this **dinosaur** lived.

Tyrannosaurus rex lived in areas that were usually warm and wet. There were lots of hills and **valleys.** There were also **volcanoes,** which sprayed smoke and ash.

A Land of Trees

fossil of a leaf

Plant **fossils** tell us which plants grew in the places where Tyrannosaurus rex lived. Scientists can also learn what the weather was like long ago by studying the plant fossils. Some plants only grew where it was warm.

Tyrannosaurus rex lived in woods and forests with many open spaces. There were pine trees and **ferns** like those that grow today. Other plants were very different from today's plants. There were no grasses.

Living with Tyrannosaurus Rex

The **fossils** of other animals tell us what they were like. Some of these animals lived at the same time as Tyrannosaurus rex.

fossil of a snake

Small **mammals** lived among the plants. The mammals ate bugs. Birds flew through the sky. Flying **reptiles,** called **pterosaurs,** looked for food as they flew. Snakes slid along the ground. **Lizards** ate plants or small animals.

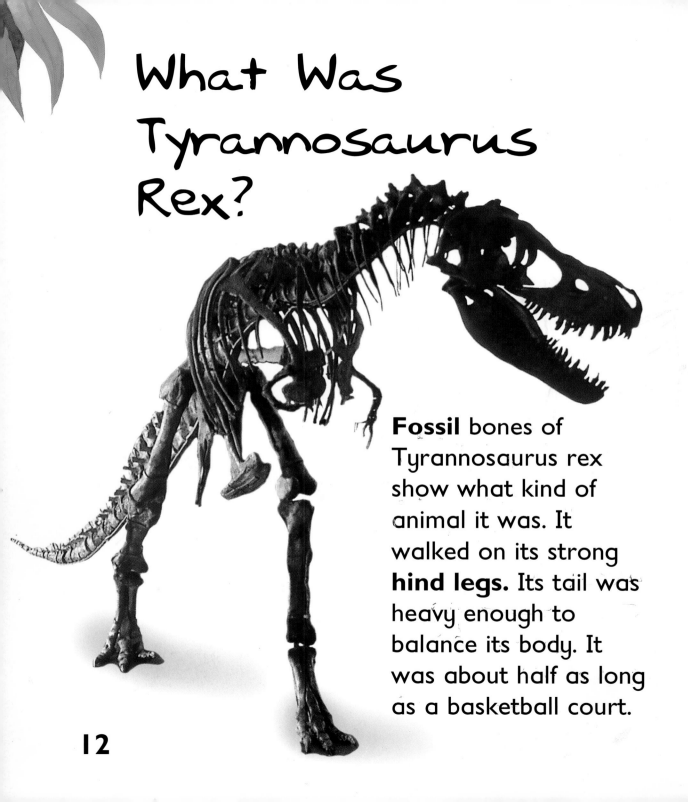

What Was Tyrannosaurus Rex?

Fossil bones of Tyrannosaurus rex show what kind of animal it was. It walked on its strong **hind legs.** Its tail was heavy enough to balance its body. It was about half as long as a basketball court.

Tyrannosaurus rex was a very powerful animal. It was one of the largest meat-eaters that ever lived. It was so heavy that the ground probably shook when it walked. It weighed as much as six elephants.

Baby Tyrannosaurus Rex

Scientists have not found any Tyrannosaurus rex eggs. They have found **fossils** from babies of other big meat-eating **dinosaurs**. These show us what Tyrannosaurus rex babies might have looked like.

dinosaur eggs

14

Their babies probably looked the same as adults, but were much smaller. They probably stayed near the nest and their mother fed them. Later, they learned how to hunt for their own food.

Growing Up

The **fossils** of some young **dinosaurs** that were like Tyrannosaurus rex have been found. They show that young animals were more **agile** and could run faster than adults.

Some scientists think that young Tyrannosaurus rex may have hunted together. They probably hunted small animals, such as **lizards.** By the time they were full-grown, they were strong enough to hunt alone.

On the Move

Tyrannosaurus rex had strong and heavy legs and hips. It had powerful muscles for walking. Swishing its tail helped Tyrannosaurus rex change direction quickly.

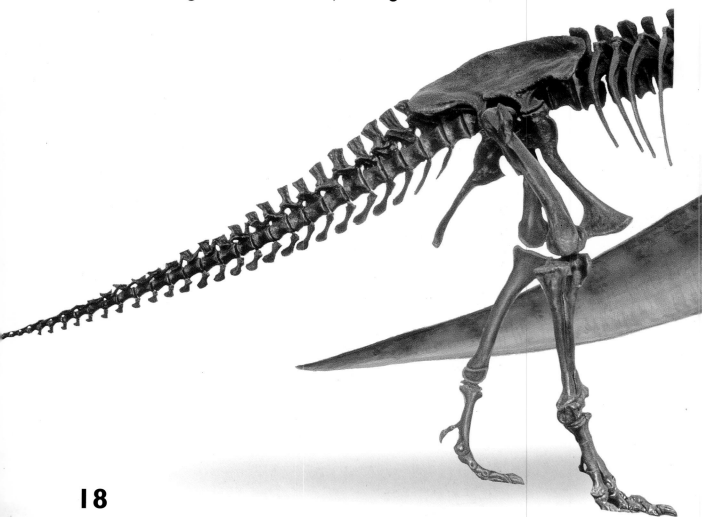

Tyrannosaurus rex walked slowly most of the time. It could run fast when it wanted to, but it would have become tired quickly. It could not run fast for long distances.

Designed to Bite

Scientists have found many Tyrannosaurus rex teeth. The teeth were different sizes. Some were as long as a pencil and were very sharp. The edges of the teeth were **jagged** like steak knives.

Tyrannosaurus rex had about 60 teeth in its jaws. These teeth were able to tear through meat easily. Tyrannosaurus rex ate other **dinosaurs.** It used its teeth to bite off chunks of meat and crush bone.

Hunting

Some scientists believe Tyrannosaurus rex hunted for food. It could open its mouth very wide, then snap it shut with strong muscles. This could have killed its **prey** with one bite.

Tyrannosaurus rex skull

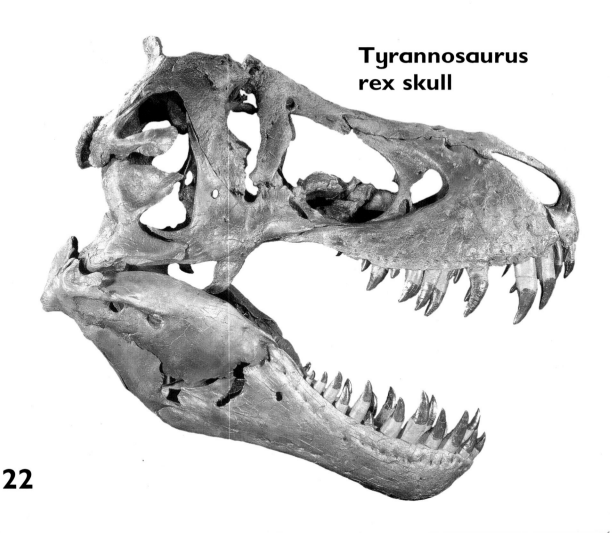

Tyrannosaurus rex may have hid in trees or bushes and waited for another **dinosaur** to come close. Then, Tyrannosaurus rex would attack its prey.

What Tyrannosaurus Rex Ate

Tyrannosaurus rex ate other **dinosaurs,** such as **hadrosaurs.** Hadrosaurs were large plant-eating dinosaurs. Some hadrosaur bones have been found with marks on them made by Tyrannosaurus rex's teeth.

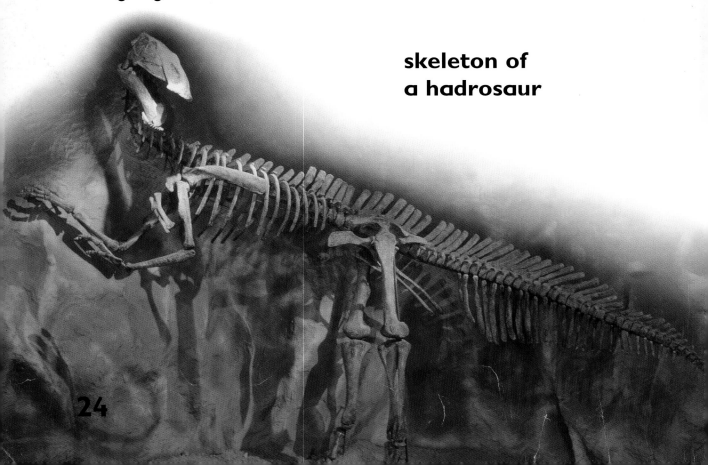

skeleton of a hadrosaur

Hadrosaurs were not as large or as strong as
Tyrannosaurus rex. They were easy **prey** for
Tyrannasaurus rex. Dozens of hadrosaur **fossils**
have been found with Tyrannosaurus rex fossils.
This shows that they lived at the same time and in
the same places.

Finding Dead Animals

Some scientists believe Tyrannosaurus rex did not hunt other **dinosaurs.** Most hunting dinosaurs used their front legs to grab hold of **prey.** But Tyrannosaurus rex had tiny front legs. It might not have been a good hunter.

These scientists think Tyrannosaurus rex fed on large dinosaurs that died of old age or disease. Tyrannosaurus rex could probably smell a dead dinosaur from a long way away. It would follow the smell and come to feast on the body.

Where Tyrannosaurus Rex Lived

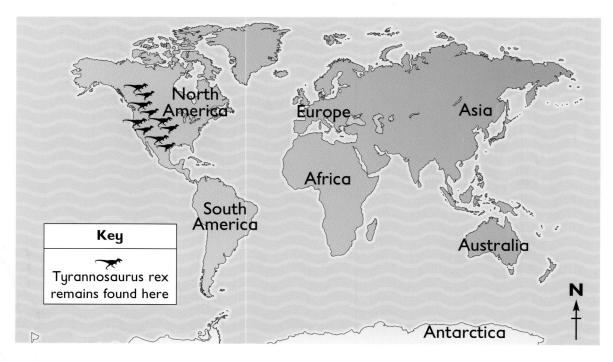

Tyrannosaurus rex lived in the western part of North America. At that time, the center of North America was covered by a large, shallow sea. Other **dinosaurs** like Tyrannosaurus rex lived millions of years earlier in North America and Asia.

When Tyrannosaurus Rex Lived

Tyrannosaurus lived for only a few million years. It lived at the very end of the Age of Dinosaurs, about 65 million years ago. Dinosaurs called Albertosaurus, Tarbosaurus, and Daspletosaurus were very similar to Tyrannosaurus rex. They lived earlier.

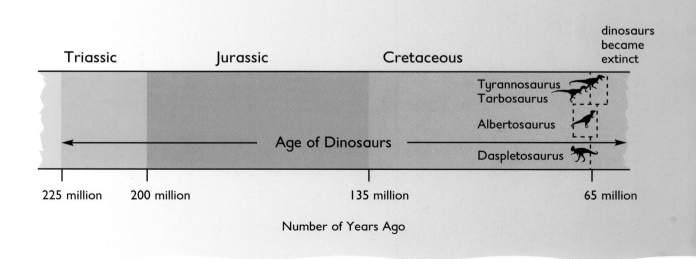

| Triassic | Jurassic | Cretaceous | dinosaurs became extinct |

Tyrannosaurus
Tarbosaurus

Albertosaurus

← Age of Dinosaurs →

Daspletosaurus

225 million   200 million   135 million   65 million

Number of Years Ago

Fact File

Tyrannosaurus rex	
Length:	up to 40 feet (12 meters)
Height:	up to 20 feet (6 meters)
Weight:	6.6 tons (6 metric tons)
Time:	Late Cretaceous Period, about 65 million years ago
Place:	North America

How to Say It

dinosaur—dine-ah-sor
hadrosaur—had-ra-sor

pterosaur—terra-sor
Tyrannosaurus rex—tah-rahn-ah-sor-us recks

Glossary

agile able to run quickly, jump, and change direction easily

dinosaur one of a large group of reptiles that lived on Earth millions of years ago

extinct no longer living on Earth

fern plant with long, curly leaves that grow from the ground

fossil remains of a plant or animal, usually found inside rocks. Most fossils are hard parts like bones or teeth. Some fossils are traces of animals, such as their footprints.

hadrosaur type of large plant-eating dinosaur that lived at the same time as Tyrannosaurus rex

hind legs back legs of an animal

jagged sharp, uneven edge

lizard small reptile with four legs that still exists today

mammal animal with hair or fur. Mammals give birth to live young instead of laying eggs.

prey animal that is hunted and eaten by another animal

pterosaur type of extinct reptile. It had wings made of skin and could fly. There were many different kinds of pterosaurs.

reptile cold-blooded animal, such as a snake or lizard

valley low area of land found between hills and mountains

volcano opening in the earth's surface where hot rocks, lava and ash come out

More Books to Read

Cohen, Daniel. *Tyrannosaurus Rex*. Mankato, Minn.: Capstone Press, Inc., 2000.

Gaines, Richard. *Tyrannosaurus Rex*. Edina, Minn: Abdo Publishing Company, 2001.

Olshevsky, George. *Tyrannosaurus Rex*. Mankato, Minn.: Smart Apple Media, 2003.

Rodriguez, K.S. *Tyrannosaurus Rex*. Austin, Tex.: Raintree Publishers, 2000.

Index